The Prayer Of A Transformed Life

Authored by:
Dr. Paul Perkins

Copyright 2014 Dr. Paul Perkins

All rights reserved. No part of this book may be reproduced in any form without written permission from the author.

ISBN-13:978-1497567474

ISBN-10:1497567475

Printed in the United States of America

This book is dedicated to family, friends, and professors who helped me in my Christian journey.

"He who is not contented with what he has would not be contented with what he would like to have." — *Socrates*

Table of Contents

Preface 5

A Dangerous Prayer: Agur, son of Jakeh 6

A Lifetime of Learning 14

Pursuit of Godly Character 28

Satisfied With Middle Class 48

If God Is All I Need, Who is the Lord? 63

Striving For Mediocrity 79

Running With The Big Dogs 94

If All I Had Were God 102

A Final Word 112

Preface

Dear Reader,

Have you ever wondered what influences our behavior? Our motivations lie deep within us, they are shaped by our experiences, the knowledge that we gather, and our positive and negative interactions with others.

Everyone struggles under the day-to-day pressures of life, but our lives don't have to be dictated them. I want my life to be meaningful, and that only comes by understanding the world as God has created it and developing a biblical worldview molded by God's perspective. I hope you find grace in these pages; that you will hear the song of God's heart as you struggle with our common experiences. My prayer is that you will join in the chorus and long for greater things in your life. Seek God and you will find Him, and through the Holy Spirit encounter a new way of living.

Striving for God's glory,

Dr. Paul Perkins

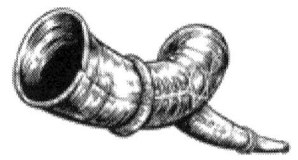

A Dangerous Prayer: Agur, son of Jakeh

Taking dangerous risks has been a part of my life: mountain climbing, skydiving, spelunking, and scuba diving in barracuda infested waters. I thrived on adventure, and the more the adrenaline pumped the better. Unless there was some risk the activity wasn't worth the effort. What drives a person to engage in such risky activities? Why would a man endanger the well being of his family for the next thrill?

At the core of an adrenaline junkie's life is the issue of discontent. The every day monotony of a mundane existence drives them to find some kind of escape and some kind of thrill. Think about your life. You get up every morning about the same time. You eat the same food on most days and it's exciting when you get pancakes on Saturday. You go to work and do the same thing you have done for years, and go home, you fall into your Lazy Boy, and turn on the television, or you pick up the latest adventure novel. Later you go to bed and in the morning you start all over again. If you're lucky you hold out for the weekend where you can do something different, something that will divert your attention from the drudgery of the week before and the week ahead.

Not everyone finds escape in the same place. Some pour their lives into their work, where the next sale or promotion is the prize, and the exhilaration of the hunt gets their heart pumping. Others find their escape by numbing their senses and indulging themselves through addictions. Extreme sports have taken ordinary activities to the edge. No longer is skateboarding a leisurely ride down a tapered drive way. If there isn't a flip, a grind, or a stunt then you're not a skateboarder. Extreme activities have become commonplace, and are now the staple of American entertainment. Shows like Fear Factor, WWF, and even the short-lived Extreme Football league were attempts to satisfy our craving for excitement. We live for reality programming because our own lives have become monotonous. The adolescent phrase "I'm bored" has crept into the adult vocabulary, and we long for something novel.

Whatever it is, it isn't new. Solomon said it four thousand years ago,

> *"So I hated life, because the work that is done under the sun was grievous to me. All of it is meaningless, a chasing after the wind."*
> *Ecclesiastes 2:17 (NIV)*

Solomon sought to understand life, and in his search he neglected nothing. He pursued every pleasure imaginable, and in the end found that it was meaningless, a striving after the wind. Today our culture has taken up Solomon's banner,

> *"I denied myself nothing my eyes desired; I refused*

my heart no pleasure." Ecclesiastes 2:10 (NIV)

The Prayer of a Searching Heart

Agur was the son of Jakeh. He is mentioned once in the Bible, Proverbs 30:1. He left us a collection of 33 verses—proverbs that God saw fit to place in the Holy Scriptures. His name is derived from the Hebrew root word, Ag, meaning hireling or collector, gatherer and he was probably a collector of proverbs. We don't know if he was contemporary with Solomon or followed after him. Either way he was familiar with Solomon's writings. In the middle of his proverbs he inserts this prayer:

> *"Two things I ask of you, O Lord; do not refuse me before I die: Keep falsehood and lies far from me; Give me neither poverty nor riches, but give me only my daily bread. Otherwise, I may have too much and disown you and say, 'Who is the Lord?' Or I may become poor and steal, and so dishonor the name of my God." Proverbs 30:7-9 (NIV)*

Agur had read the words of Solomon. He had seen the excessive efforts of the wisest man of Israel, and found them to be a warning to a generation of hedonistic discontents. In the midst of his own reflections, Agur asks God to give him, before he died, a life that was not shaped by his culture, but one that was totally dependent on God. Agur wanted to shed the weight of a prosperity bent society seeking wealth for its own sake and neglected to rest in the provision of Jehovah Jira.

This is an extraordinary message for the church of our century! We have bought into the fast paced, production oriented, climb our way to the top mentality. We have lost our way and desperately need to be led gently back to an understanding of God's heart. What would happen in our culture if the church prayed Agur's prayer? How would the people in our churches respond if we told them to lighten up and slow down?

A Call To A Different Life

So, why write a book about Agur's prayer? As a pastor of over 25 years I placed a lot of effort into building a ministry, and I knew all the right verses and pithy sayings. *"It's not me that builds the house, but God." "I am only planting and watering, but it's God who gives the increase." "Unless the Lord builds the house we labor in vain."* Yet, every time I walked into the church, a home, or a hospital I felt the weight of the lives I touched. The couple sitting in front of me didn't want to hear that I had no answers for them, or that they needed to trust only in God. They wanted their marriage fixed, children obedient, and food on the table. When they were sitting in the hospital and a family member was in pain they wanted the pastor. Whether they expected me to perform a miracle or not, I felt the burden of their pain and wished I could make everything better.

The church down the street had better programs, more cars in the parking lot, and bigger buildings. I feared that the people in my congregation would find out and switch churches. I couldn't make people go to church, join a small group, or want to be discipled. Yet, if the numbers sagged, or people felt left out, or there wasn't any spiritual growth — the buck stopped here. So, as any responsible pastor would do I turned it on the congregation and sermons about working harder, commitment, and reaching out rang from the pulpit. People were admonished, cajoled, and made to feel guilty so that they would be involved, increase production and make me feel better. I turned to the leaders of the church and pressed them to produce lest the wrath of the congregation come on them with the question, "What are you doing about this?" And the cycle continued.

Whether you are a pastor, elder or deacon, or a person in the pew you need to hear Agur's prayer. For in his words are found the secret to a successful life. There is no magic formula or golden parachute, but rather a changed heart. If this is what you want then keep on reading.

Further Reflection

1. Are you discontent, why?

2. How do you feel pressured into a cycle of performance?

3. How have you contributed to a worldview of production spirituality?

4. If you could change one thing about your life what would it be?

    Transformation begins when we submit our way of thinking to God's. As our understanding of God's will permeates our lives we realize that what is truly important has been achieved for us in Christ and we are free to receive all the blessings of God.

A Lifetime of Learning

"Two things I ask of you, O Lord; do not refuse me before I die:"

An old American proverb states, *"There is nothing certain but death and taxes."* Two pictures spring to mind when I think of this proverb. The first comes every year like clockwork. I pull out all my W-2's and receipts and painstakingly do my taxes. The second picture is my brother standing in the National Cemetery in Florida contemplating life and death as he reads the names of our father and mother.

Two pictures, one that happens every year and the other that happens only once, and the latter is most excruciating. The reason it is harder is because, unlike taxes, it is the one that is certain. I can escape some of the pain of taxes, but death is inevitable. The Apostle Paul said,

> *"Therefore, just as sin entered the world through one man, and death through Sin, and in this way death came to all men, because all sinned" (Romans 5:12 NIV).*

The writer of Hebrews puts it this way, *"Just as man is destined to die once..." (Hebrews 9:27 NIV).*

Ever since Adam and Eve's disobedience in the garden death has come to all men. Every day we are faced with our immortality; whether the funeral of a two year old or a ninety-nine year old the outcome is the same. No one likes to face the fact of a limited existence, but as Solomon reminds us,

> *"As it is with the good man, so with the sinner; as it is with those who take oaths, so with those who are afraid to take them... The same destiny overtakes all   (death)"* (Ecclesiastes

9:2b, 3b NIV).

Agur understood this as he prayed, *"do not refuse me before I die."* He could hear his old teacher's advice ringing in his ears, *"for it is now that God favors what you do." (Ecclesiastes 9:7b NIV).* Unless you are Enoch or Elijah life is limited and we must seek the Lord and His favor now. We must ask Him to grant us our requests that we might live lives that are worthy of being called children of God.

Tyler was out with his friends. The evening passed without incident as they laughed, danced, and drank. When the time came for them to leave he staggered slightly into the dark, finding his motorcycle near the entrance to the bar. His friends passed and gave no notice to his condition as he straddled his bike and roared off down the street.

He drove too fast, too late, and too inebriated. Hundreds of students and adults came to his funeral. He was popular, but he was not invincible. A life full of possibilities abruptly halted in one foolish act. Death comes to us all and sometimes when we least expect it.

God will not always be available to us. *"Seek the Lord while he may be found; call on him while he is near" (Isaiah 55:6 NIV).* His desire is for us to call on Him, and seek Him with all our heart, and why? Because He knows that there is a limited amount of time. Each of us has a finite number of days, days that are written in the books of God. The problem is that we don't know the number. So, it is important for us to seek God now, because once our spirit is released from this body we will stand before Him and be held accountable for the life that we have lived.

A friend of mine prayed years for her husband. Her life was exemplary and he liked her friends. On occasion he would even attend church activities, but he didn't think he needed to believe in Jesus. His heart began to change when he came face-to-face with his mortality and was diagnosed with cancer. We shared the gospel with him, prayed with him, and read scripture with him, and though he was receptive he would not yield his heart. The night before his death I sat in the hospital room and talked to him about seeking God when he could be found. I explained that once he died there were no other opportunities, and in his final hours he submitted his heart to Jesus and was eventually ushered into his Savior's presence. The Father gives us every opportunity to respond to his call, but there is a time when He won't listen, and that is when death steals the moment away.

"Do not refuse me before I die."

Pride provokes our attempts to control the uncertainties of life. The Scriptures says,

> *"Now listen, you who say, 'today or tomorrow we will go to this or that city, spend a year there, carry on business and make money.' Why, you don't even know what will happen tomorrow. What is your life? You are a mist that appears for a little while and then vanishes" (James 4:13,14 NIV).*

Even though there is little in this life we can control, we work hard to give the impression that we are life's masters. Jesus told a parable in Luke 12:13-21 about a man of great wealth. The man produced an abundance of crops, but found himself without storage space for his grain. He said to himself, *"This is what I will do. I will tear down my barns and build bigger ones, and there I will store all my grain and my goods" (vs. 18 NIV).* He had his life and future under control. He could sit back and enjoy life, with enough money to send his children to college, pay off his mortgage, take a cruise, and even retire early.

In 2008 my wife and I were on top of the world. We owned a beautiful home, sent the youngest two off to college, and had enough money to do pretty much whatever we wanted. Then it happened. I lost my job and the economy tanked. We had to use our retirement money to pay our creditors, and we lost a bundle on the sale of our home. Like many Americans we had put too much stock in the stability of the American Dream.

Yet, God said to

him, *"You fool! This very night your life will be demanded from you. Then you will get what you have prepared for yourself"* (vs. 20 NIV).

> **"Two things I ask of you, O Lord;
> do not refuse me before I die."**

Agur knew that there was something more to this life and he didn't want it to pass him by, and he wanted the Lord to grant him his prayer so that he would find favor with Him before his death.

The Long Obedience

There is something else that lies beneath the surface of Agur's request, something that begs our attention. We don't know his age at the time he wrote his prayer, we don't know if he was lying on his deathbed, or if he was a young man whose heart was turned toward God. In the NIV proverbs 30:1 reads, *"This man declares".* The word 'the' is a definite article in the Hebrew and literally states, "The man". The phrase would not have been used of a young man, but rather one who had life experience and had gained some wisdom. I think Agur was in his middle age. He had left the foolishness of youth, and in wisdom looked past the present, and longed for a better future.

This is a perspective that can only come with age. Youth worry less about dying because they believe their whole future is before them. They think they are invincible and indulge in the pleasures of the present instead of looking toward the future. It's a double edge sword. We need to understand our mortality so that we can give proper attention to the future.

Not only did Agur's request reflect his understanding of man's mortality, but it also can be seen as an illustration for how he wanted to live his life. It could be paraphrased like this,

> *"Lord, I know I am mortal and one day I am going to die. Before this happens I ask that you build the following things into my life."*

He knew that wisdom didn't come over night, and that godly character took time. It was a request that

God would continually work in his heart. There is a difference between a presumptive heart bent on pleasing itself without regard to God's plans, and a heart that realized that life was short, and in whatever length he had left, wanted God to be at work. The process of allowing God to work in our lives is called sanctification.

Paul said, *"[Be] confident in this, that he who began a good work in you will carry it on to completion until the day of Christ Jesus"* (Philippians 1:6 NIV).

Followers of Jesus have the assurance that God's work isn't finished, and that He desires to conform us into the image of His Son. God has invested heavily in his reclamation program. Jesus gave His life so that we can enter into the presence of the Father. Jesus' resurrection displayed God's power over sin and death, and the sending of the Holy Spirit is the seal of His promise.

God's investment, however, comes with obligations, and we are to reciprocate by investing in God. Paul balances God's work and our effort,

"Therefore, my dear friends, as you have always obeyed—not only in my presence, but now much more in my absence—continue to work out your salvation with fear and trembling, for it is God who works in you to will and to act according to his good purpose" (Philippians 2:12,13 NIV).

Our salvation needs to be worked out. That is, since we are saved we need to conform our lives to the reality of our salvation. We can't just sit back as if we haven't any responsibility to obey.

A couple in our church was having difficulties in their marriage. His wife came to my wife for counsel, and as a result I called him up and made an appointment to see him. He readily admitted that their marriage was in trouble, but he wasn't doing anything about it. He was praying that God would do something, and he was waiting. I commended him for praying because that is where we need to start. But if it weren't for his wife seeking counsel their marriage would have ended. I told him this was his answer to prayer, and now it was time for him to do some work.

We cannot neglect our need to be obedient. The other side of Paul's admonition was that even though we are to be at work, it is God who is at work in us. As we daily yield our will to His, He is able to mold our character and behavior to conform to the image of His Son, but it is not an overnight event.

Since becoming a believer in 1975 I have found that God seldom leads in a straight line. My spiritual growth has been a steady incline, but I have had my ups and downs. My desire to live and become all that God wants for me has often been two steps forward, one step back. I have seen the greatest gains in my faith when I realize that what I do in this life for God is more important than anything else. It is amazing how God brings people along in their spiritual walk. For some progress is with leaps and bounds. They seem to have the spiritual energy of ten life times. For others it is much slower, gradual, and sometimes very painful. But to each of us God gives His abundant grace at the right time.

Running the race isn't a sprint, but a marathon, and marathon's can be agonizing. I have some young friends who take to the streets every year to run excruciatingly long races. At the end they are sweaty, cramped, and exhausted—but they finished. The finish line, however, couldn't have been crossed if they hadn't put the time in to increase their endurance. They built up gradually, running small distances first and increasing it until their bodies where in tune with their task.

The other extreme was my brother. We lived in Turkey while in High School, and wanting to be a part of the athletics program he tried out for track and field, specifically long distance. He seemed to do well until we competed against a school in the mountains. The higher altitude made breathing harder, and my brother was a smoker. Running came easy for him, and he didn't see the need to get rid of the hindrances that could keep him from winning. He finished last because he was not prepared.

The same can be said of the spiritual life. It is a marathon, where we learn incrementally to trust in Christ and the goodness of God. As we persevere in the small things greater things are given, and when we finish we can look back and see the distance we have come to the praise of the Father. However, we need to constantly prepare ourselves by pursing God and throwing off hindrances.

> *"Let us throw off everything that hinders and the sin that so easily entangles. And let us run with perseverance the race marked out for us (Hebrew 12:1 NIV).*

I don't know how much time I have left on this earth. With all the reports of cancer, natural disasters, crime, and accidents tomorrow could prove the vanishing of this simple mist. So, with Agur, I ask that God, in the time that I have remaining, grant me my request.

"Two things I ask of you, O Lord; do not refuse me before I die"

Further Reflection

1. How has death touched your life?

2. How did the person's death change the way you think about living?

3. How would you feel toward God if all your possessions were taken away?

4. How have you treated your spiritual life more like a sprint?

5. What hindrances do you to need let go in order for God to have supremacy in you life?

Pray that God will open your heart to his perspective of life and death. Grieve if you have lost a love one and ask God's compassion to overwhelm you. Throw off any sin and ask forgiveness. Thank the Lord for his compassionate mercy.

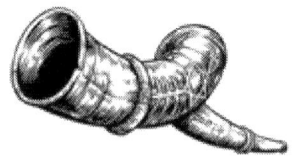

Pursuit of Godly Character

Keep Falsehood and lies far from me

Lying comes naturally to children. The first time they get into mischief a defense mechanism kicks in and they will do almost anything to keep from getting into trouble. If the pain of punishment looms greater than the potential pain of getting caught, children (dare I say adults as well) will lie in hopes they will escape punishment, and be free from pain. Of course when they get away with little lies the bigger ones become easier.

I know this firsthand. In grade school lying was easier than telling the truth. It was habitual even though most of the time I got caught. Third grade spelling was never easy for me, and with each failing test I had to get a parental signature to show that they reviewed my work. I didn't want to face the pain of my parents' discipline so, with the help of my brother; I learned to forge my mom's name. It really wasn't a good forgery and each time I got caught and had to face the consequences of both the bad spelling test, and being deceitful. The teacher would give me 'licks' with the paddle, and my mom with the shower shoe. In my sin I was determined to win this fight and the lying continued.

Fast forward to high school. I was working for a law firm as a legal runner, and my job was to file documents at the courthouse. Occasionally I did odd jobs around the office, and since the office was being remodeled I was asked to do painting after hours. I said yes even though I really didn't want to be there. One evening I was painting the trim along the ceiling, and my elbow bumped the can of paint sitting on the top rung of the ladder. It fell to the ground spilling its contents on the brand new carpet. So I did what any normal high-school student would do--I panicked and left. I didn't call anyone; I didn't leave a note; I just left.

The next morning I received a call from one of the partners of the law firm asking about the spilled paint. I was faced with a dilemma. Telling the truth might mean losing my job, paying for the damage, or humiliation for not having the sense to call someone. A good lie might keep me out of trouble all together. I did what came natural to me. I told him I fell from the ladder and hit my head. I was knocked out for a couple of minutes and when I woke I stumbled out and went home.

Those lawyers were smart. They had to have seen through the lie, but not one of them said anything to me. I kept my job and was not held accountable for the cost of cleaning up the mess. Allowing my deceit to go unchallenged, even if their actions were an act of grace and mercy, reinforced the idea that a good lie is better than the truth.

The Father Of Lies

Agur understood that a life of godly character was marked by an ability to hold to the truth and refrain from falsehood.

Keep me from falsehood and lies

He knew that if he were to exhibit a life of received blessing he would need to follow the truth and not the lies. Jesus talking to the Pharisees said,

> *"You belong to your father, the devil, and you want to carry out your father's desires. He was a murderer from the beginning, not holding to the truth, for there is no truth in him. When he lies, he speaks his native language, for he is a liar and the father of lies" (John 8:44 NIV).*

In order for us to live a life of truth and not falsehood we need to know our enemy. Satan is a liar. He was a liar in the beginning, he is a liar now, and he will always be a liar. His aim is to foil the plan of God, and his best weapon is his lies. It is his nature and, as such, nothing he dangles in front of us will be for our good, and will only bring destruction and heartache.

When Jesus was going through His temptations in the wilderness, the father of lies approached him with biblical truth. Satan twisted the scriptures for his own use, to try and lead astray the Son of God and bring all authority under his control. The scriptures say that Satan masquerades as an angel of light (2 Cor. 11:14), coming to us as a friend, with an outstretched hand, a kind look, offering gifts of pleasure, power, and wealth. All the while his only desire is to deceive us into following after him, drawing us away from God, and ruining our lives.

The Great Deception

Here is a profound statement, ***when you are deceived you don't realize it.*** If you knew that you were being deceived there would be no deception because you would understand it to be a lie. Lies are always set in opposition to truth. When we know the truth lies are exposed for the destructiveness they bring. So, if we have the truth why do we so willingly lie? That's a good question. We could say it is because of our sinful nature, but that is an easy out. Adam and Eve didn't have a sinful nature, they lived in harmony with God (the source of truth), and they were still deceived.

Eve was at a crossroads. God had set out the parameters of her life, and she could have anything in the garden she wanted, just not from one tree. The deceiver saw how her curiosity caused her to walk past the tree and allowed her gaze to linger, to ask the unspoken question, "what is it about this tree that makes it so different from the others?"

One day, as Eve was passing by the tree, the deceiver began to spin his web of deceit, questioning her about God's prohibition, casting doubt in her mind and then offering her something that, it seemed, God wanted to keep from her.

"When the woman saw that the fruit of the tree

> *was good for food and pleasing to the eye, and also desirable for gaining wisdom, she took some and ate it" (Gen. 3:6).*

The Apostle John writing thousands of years later put it this way,

> *"For everything in the world--the cravings of sinful man, the lust of his eyes and the boasting of what he has and does--comes not from the Father but from the world" (1 John 2:16).*

The Cravings of Sinful Man

Every appetite is God given and good. He created us to enjoy life, to have pleasure, and to know Him. There is nothing that we feel or desire that doesn't have its roots in the goodness of God. That is not to say that what we do with these desires is pleasing to Him. Whenever we go our way instead of God's we find ourselves outside of His blessings. Eve saw the fruit and believed the lie of the serpent. She allowed him to cast doubt on God's truth and she began to believe the lie, and was deceived. Man has perverted the good desires of God and made them into destructive behaviors.

All addictions fall into this category. The purity of sex has become perverted in pornography, prostitution, homosexuality, bestiality, and all other sorts of bizarre behavior. The desire to be filled with God has been perverted by people trying to find answers at the bottom of a bottle, the point of a syringe, or popping pills. The appetites of our stomachs replace the hunger for righteousness and peace with God. We indulge ourselves to excess for the pure pleasure of eating. The Romans used to eat till they could eat no more, vomit, and eat again. *"For such people are not serving our Lord Christ, but their own appetites"* (Romans 16:18 NIV).

Sin has been explained away by an unbelieving world. They claim we are animals, so our children can't help but to act on their sexual impulses, and genetics has excused homosexuality, alcoholism, and violent behavior. Paul describes it this way, *"They exchanged the truth of God for a lie...Because of this, God gave them over to shameful lusts"* (Romans 1:25a, 26a).

The cravings of the flesh are the uninhibited expression of our physical appetites without regard to the truth of God. When we allow ourselves to become controlled by these desires then we are no better than animals, but we are not animals. Yet, when men, created in the image of God, turn away from God's truth, giving themselves over to their appetites they begin to look for ways to express these lusts outwardly.

The Lust Of The Eyes

Materialistic evolution says that as man rose from the dust of self-indulgence he began to look outside of his basic needs to satisfy something greater. He looked around not only at what could satisfy him physically, but he now saw a world he could conquer. We observe that man doesn't stop at satisfying his daily needs. He is driven beyond the necessities of life to accumulate (we will talk about this later). For right now we want to briefly look at the deception that Satan has placed before us. It is the same deception that was dangled in front of Jesus in the desert. "Bow to me," Satan said to Jesus, "and I will give you the kingdoms of the world" (Matthew 4 NIV). Wealth, power, and control were in Jesus' grasp if only He worshipped Satan. Sounds tempting, but Satan doesn't offer me the world, rather he offers me things that entice my heart and desire. He says, *"I will give you a bigger church, a larger salary, more responsibility and control if you will only compromise, talk less about the blood of Jesus, expect less of the people."*

Haven't you ever thought about how much more you could purchase if you didn't tithe? Think about it; you could have that new car, a bigger house, better clothes or furniture if only you didn't give to the church. Our culture is built on the lust of the eyes, the desire to have more than we need. We have instant food, instant credit, and instant coffee. We have throwaway plates, throw away contacts, and throw away spouses. Our lust for new and better destroys relationships. Our lust for power leaves broken people in our wake. Our lust for control leads us to dominate our family and friends.

God told Adam to subdue the earth, and having dominion over creation is a natural part of our existence. But the lust for more is beyond dominion. It is the subjugation of every thing possible for the pure pleasure of domination. As Captain Jack Sparrow said in the Pirates of the Caribbean, "Take what you can and give nothing back."

Whether it is a Hitler or Saddam Hussein who wants to control the world, or just me who wants to control the lives of the people in my sphere of influence, everyone is guilty of the lust of the eyes. We only see what we want and take it without any concern for others.

The Pride of Life

"The woman saw that the fruit was good...also desirable for gaining wisdom."

The idea that I can gain enough knowledge to

control my destiny has not changed over the centuries. The serpent tempted Eve in the garden and appealed to her curiosity saying that God was keeping something from her. He suggested that if she disobeyed the Creator that she could acquire wisdom beyond her imagination. *"You can be as God, knowing good and evil,"* the serpent told her. We have been cast into this downward spiral ever since, and still believe that if we can gain enough knowledge we can get ourselves out of any predicament.

Before the enlightenment, the general understanding was that searching for knowledge was an attempt to know God. However, with the coming of the enlightenment, knowledge was a way to assert ones self beyond God. The more man learned the less he needed a deity. In the twentieth century education became the savior of man, and it was thought possible to rid the world of disease, corruption, and 'sin' by acquiring more knowledge. Educated people would rise above hatred and poverty. The intelligencia would be able to direct the ignorant toward a utopia.

But what happened? Scientists found that as one disease was cured another more deadly took its place. Governments found that advancement in technology gave rise to more powerful ways to express our hate. Society found that science wasn't sufficient enough to answer the questions of meaning and purpose. Yet, even in all this man won't turn to God. He finds himself mired in the bog of his own pride.

Recently I saw this played out in a debate between a Christian Scientist and an Atheistic Scientist. No matter what evidence was produced by the Christian, the atheist would not give ground. He was awed by the universe and blinded to its Creator. He believed in the limitless capacity of man to expand his learning, but ignored the possibility of a limitless God. His pride in mans intellectual possibility kept him from comprehending an all knowing God.

Paul described it to Timothy like this,

"There will be terrible times in the last days. People will be lovers of themselves, lovers of

money, boastful, proud, abusive, disobedient to their parents, ungrateful, unholy, without love, unforgiving, slanderous, without self-control...always learning but never able to acknowledge the truth" (2 Timothy 3:1-7 NIV).

The world will be proud and boastful, always learning but never acknowledging the truth. What a statement about modern culture. We have become so confident in our capacity to acquire knowledge that we have dismissed God's Word as being relevant, and the logical conclusion is to dismiss God Himself.

Speaking The Truth

So what is the answer to the deceiver and his deceptions? JESUS! That sounds simplistic and I don't want to give a false impression about the difficulties of life. But in every difficult situation, in every tragedy, in every valley of existence Jesus brings hope. So, we are to battle the lies of the evil one by knowing the author of life -- Jesus.

"...[We] may be built up until we all reach unity in the faith and in the knowledge of the Son of God...then we will no longer be infants, tossed back and forth by the waves, and blown here and there by every wind of teaching and by the cunning and craftiness of men in their deceitful scheming. Instead, speaking the TRUTH in love, we will in all things grow up into him who is the Head, that is, Christ." (Ephesians 4:2-15)

The greatest deception of them all, and it started in the garden, is that we don't need God. It is when we come to know the truth, that God has made Himself available to us through His Son Jesus, that we can let down the barriers that keep us from living the life that God has created us to live. Jesus said, *"I am the way, the truth, and the life"* (John 14:6 NIV). He is the only way to God; He embodies the only truth of God's will, and in Christ God gives both abundant life now and eternal life in the future.

Agur realized that to get a good look at the God

of Israel, God was going to have to keep him clear of the falsehoods that blind men. The temptation is to find the answers to life's questions, not in God's will, but in our own ability to sort things out. God gave us a mind, yes, to understand our environment, to learn about Him and each other, to better enjoy life, but He never gave us these faculties to be exercised apart from Him. When we use our mind, our knowledge, and our wisdom in concert with His will we are able to live life to the fullest.

    A long time friend posted that she had enough. She said, "I don't love him any more. I spent the last ten years of my life meeting everyone else's needs, now it's my turn. God wants me happy doesn't he, so why should I stay in this marriage? I need me time." She was ready to throw away ten years of marriage to find herself, but she was doing it outside of God's revealed will. It took a while, but through the gentle prodding of friends and the Holy Spirit she returned home and she and her husband sought help.

    The attitude reminds me of the Tobi Keith song *I*

Want To Talk About Me,

> I wanna talk about me
> Wanna talk about I
> Wanna talk about number one
> Oh my me my
> What I think, what I like, what I know, what I want,
> what I see
> I like talking about you, usually, but occasionally
> I wanna talk about me
> I wanna talk about me

American culture has bought into the narcissistic lie that happiness is when it is all about me. But God's truth says something different. We are most happy when God is most glorified, and God is most glorified in our joyful obedience. Happiness and contentment is best achieved when we follow the promises God has laid out for us, and sacrificially serve others' needs over our own.

This isn't permission for abuse, but rather an invitation to see others as opportunities for service.

When couples, children, workers, neighbors, friends, and employers follow God's principles for better living happiness will always result. Sin is the joy killer. We think that we can find peace beyond God's boundaries and when we do sin and destruction always follow. Just ask Adam and Eve.

If we truly believe what God says in His word then as we go through life and face its difficulties and joys, we should constantly place them in the context of His will. Those who have turned their backs on God face their own issues, and we can gently point them to the foot of the cross--to the grace of God. But we need to be patient, knowing that God's grace was poured out on us in the depravity of our own hearts. Jude said,

> *"Keep yourselves in God's love as you wait for the mercy of our Lord Jesus Christ to bring you to eternal life. Be merciful to those who doubt; snatch others from the fire and save them; to others show mercy, mixed with fear--hating even the clothing stained by corrupted flesh" (Jude 21 and 22 NIV).*

Don't allow pride to lift you past the throne of grace. Remember from where God has brought you and where He is taking you. Along the way let's bring others with us, and share with them the truth in love. May we be marked with the character that God wants to build into our lives, and not be deceived. May God answer our prayer,

> **"Two things I ask of you, O Lord; do not refuse me before I die; Keep falsehood and lies far from me"**

Further Reflection

1. What natural and good appetite teeters on becoming sinful?

2. What lust tempts you away from following God?

3. What lies of the world plague you the most?

4. What fear tempts you to seek answers apart from Christ?

5. What do you need to do to find a right standing with God?

6. How have you let pride keep you from God's best for you?

?

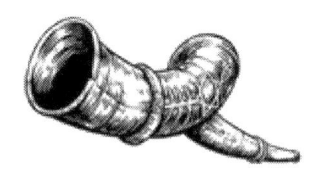

Satisfied With Middle Class

"Give me neither poverty nor riches"

Agur knew something about being content with God, to be satisfied with Him alone. His prayer went against the philosophy of his day just as it does in our own. We have bought into the idea of that the American dream is normative, but what is the American dream?

In the 1950's, post World War II, the United States was rebuilding itself and the American dream. It looked like _Leave It To Beaver_ and consisted of one wife, two kids, a nice house in the suburbs, and a dog in the back yard. Before the war the dream was out of reach for most people. The Depression had left many praying for their next meal, hoping that they would just survive.

However, with the war the economy boomed, people had jobs, and life promised hope. The American dream was alive -- and more people then ever could achieve it.

Yet, people are never satisfied, and over the years the American dream has changed. It isn't the hope of a middle class life style achieved by hard work and determination. Now it is the dream to be rich, achieved by hard work or better by pure luck. Shows like "Who Wants To Be A Millionaire" or the abundance of casinos and lottery tickets give every American the opportunity to grasp the golden ring. Akuna Matata -- No worries.

As an assistant school administrator at a small Christian School in Dallas, Texas, I met a woman who was very wealthy. She lived in a home with a mortgage of ten thousand dollars a month. As we talked she admitted that there were some satisfying things about being wealthy, but there was the down side as well. Most evenings she and her children huddled in one of the upstairs rooms for fear that someone would break in and do them harm. That may be an extreme, but it illustrates that wealth does not always bring security. Lottery winners often ostracize family and friends, and frequently the divorce court is the fruit of their abundance. Wealth is alluring, but what is wrong with affluence? Not everyone who is wealthy hides in their bedrooms or divorces their spouses.

The Root Of All Kinds of Evil

Communism and socialism see capitalism and its allure of personal wealth as the root of evil. Wealth is the devil and money is its weapon. Their philosophy of social/economic/ financial equality is inviting in the face of the one percent who seem to flaunt their wealth and deprive others of the American dream. The Scripture says,

> *"People who want to get rich fall into temptation and a trap and into many foolish and harmful desires that plunge men into ruin and destruction. For the love of money is a root of all kinds of evil. Some people, eager for money, have wandered*

from the faith and pierced themselves with many griefs" (1 Timothy 6:10 NIV).

Paul, however, does not say that money is the root of evil, but rather the love of it tempts man and leads him to destruction. The person who has to have more, no matter the reason, walks this wide road. People who grew up in poverty are often obsessed with attaining wealth. Their poverty was hard and they are determined to have a better life for themselves and their children. There is nothing wrong with wanting to provide a better life for your family, but if doing so becomes an obsession it will lead to a skewed view of life.

A friend of mine had the goal of becoming a millionaire by the time he was thirty. His aim was to work hard, save, and eventually sit back and let his money work for him. His family became the victim of his obsession. He worked late, traveled more, and when they needed him the most he wasn't there. Eventually he saw the destruction and exchanged his dream of wealth for the riches of heaven.

Others seek wealth as a means of control and power. The proverbial saying *money is power* has truth to it. For those who have felt out of control and oppressed, wealth becomes a way of regaining control. Finally, there are some who see it as a game, as a way of achieving leisure or a distraction from the harsh realities of life. They want an escape from responsibility and their wealth allows them to try one adventure after another.

Wealth can blind people to what is truly important. The accumulation of toys and the keeping up with the Jones's distracts us from what God wants us to do. Think about Jesus' story of the rich fool. There was an argument between two men whose father had died. The man who approached Jesus saw his wisdom and knew that he would judge fairly. This is what Jesus said,

> *"Watch out! Be on your guard against all kinds of greed; a man's life does not consist in the*

> *abundance of his possessions" (Luke 12:15).*

What value is there if you gain the whole world and lose your soul? All you have to do is look at Job and his life. He was a man of great wealth and prestige. God had blessed him. He lived the kind of life that everyone strives for, wealth, family, honor among his friends, and a right relationship with God. But what do the Scriptures say?

> *"Naked I came from my mother's womb, and naked I will depart" (Job 1:21a).*

Job had it all and lost it all. God allowed Satan to test him by taking away the outward necessities of life, and if Job were to survive it would rest on his faith in God alone. We don't know if or when our possessions will be taken away. What we do know is that without a confident relationship with God, through Christ Jesus, we will fall in the end.

This principle became a reality for me when in 2008 when we lost everything. As I said before we took retirement to pay debt, lost money on our house, and I didn't have a job. My first reaction was to cry "Why me God?" It took a while to refocus my priorities and allow God to be my sole source of peace and contentment. It is easy to allow the world to creep in and supplant God's priorities.

That I Might Not Forget

What are you rich toward? That was Agur's concern. He didn't want to stand before God on the Day of Judgment and find that he was rich with material possessions and poor toward the things of heaven. He didn't want to be like the rich fool who said in his heart that he didn't need God. The blessings he had received blinded him, and he began to think that he was the source of his wealth. Did he work hard? Yes. Didn't he go out in the fields and bring in the harvest? Yes. Didn't he think of building the barns so that he would secure his future? Yes, but he neglected to realize that all good gifts are from God.

God is not opposed to planning for the future. In fact He is a God who plans. Since the foundation of the world Jesus knew He would give His life. God showed Joseph that there would be a drought for three years so he could prepare and save his people. It's not that God is against solid financial planning. What God abhors is a person He blesses forgetting its source. Isn't that the heart of Agur's prayer concerning wealth?

> *"Give me neither poverty nor riches, but give me only my daily bread. Otherwise, I may have too much and disown you and say, 'who is the Lord?"*

Wealth breeds dependence amnesia; we forget to trust God. Even good religious people, who go to church, give their money, and say good things about God, can turn their hearts away from him. They view God and the church in economic terms, *"What can the church do for me,"* or *"How does the church make me feel?"* And if the terms of agreement aren't met they go to another church where their money can buy them more goods and services. They have forgotten God in their hearts—they have left their first love.

Never To Dishonor Your Name

The other extreme is not the answer either. In the Middle Ages priests took vows of poverty to express their piety before God. Even today people commit their lives to poverty so the world will not distract them from being effective for God. But this isn't what Agur was praying when he asked not to receive wealth. He knew that being poor had its traps as well.

The poor don't see their economic situation as a blessing; rather they blame God for His inattention to their American dream. They don't see it as a blessing, but a curse. In fact, most religious cultures view people in poverty as forgotten by God. They believe He has removed His blessing, but that isn't the case at all. God is the champion of the poor, and in the Old Testament Law He instructed the nation of Israel to provide for those less fortunate.

Yet, when a culture characterizes the poor as lazy, uneducated, and god-forsaken sinners without worth, the poor will do anything to establish their worth. Agur prayed that God would keep him from being poor so that he would not steal and in doing so dishonor God's name.

Petty theft, drug running, gambling, prostitution, and pornography are all ways that some people in poverty choose to find their success. They are either at the top running the shots or at the bottom being used, but they are all the same, looking for the golden parachute. They are trying to find that one opportunity that will pull them out of their financial despair.

Of course, their highest end in life isn't to glorify or honor God. But ours, as believers in Jesus Christ, is to live for God's glory. Therefore, when tempted with financial expediency, how do we respond? Are we all too ready to cheat on our income tax? Are we willing to forgo our tithe to God? Are we disposed to commit fraud, break the law, side step morality, and do whatever it takes to get by?

In the Disney movie *Aladdin* the opening scene has Aladdin stealing food because he is hungry. He sings, *"I gotta eat to live, gotta steal to eat, talk to you about it when I got the time."* Sure it's wrong, but wrong can be right under the right circumstances. That's the way our world thinks, but it isn't the way God thinks. He wants us to depend on Him. He wants us to be content with His blessings.

Agur understood his own nature and how difficult it was to be so poor that stealing seemed to be the only way out. So his prayer was simple, *"God, meet my daily needs."* However, what we think is our daily needs may be different than what God sees as our daily needs, therefore, we need the wisdom to know the difference.

The Issue Of Contentment

> "The man who fears God will avoid all extremes" (Ecclesiastes 7:18b NIV).

Solomon saw it all, the great poverty of his people and their great wealth, and he knew both were meaningless. They were extremes to avoid because neither produced godly fruit -- the fruit of contentment. Paul said,

> *"But godliness with contentment is great gain. For we brought nothing into the world, and we can take nothing out it" (1 Timothy 6:6,7 NIV).*

One of the secrets to godliness is contentment with the things that God has given us, but contentment runs contrary to our culture. American capitalism fosters an environment of discontent, breeding dissatisfied lives. Satisfaction with what God gives is seen as stagnant, poorly motivated, or not interested in seeing God's work grow. People look at you funny if you tell them you don't need another raise because you have what you need. They wonder what is wrong or maybe you have had a head injury.

One of the greatest deceptions of our time is the health and wealth movement among Christians. It has created an entitlement attitude among believers, perverting our status as God's children. Surely, God doesn't want second best for the children of the King? Illustrations are enumerated of God's promises to Israel of wealth and prosperity, and are we not grafted into those promises?

The problem is that the Old Testament promises to Israel were national promises not personal ones. The kingdom would flourish and the wealth of the nation would flood in if Israel obeyed God's commandments. There would be wealthy and poor among the people of God, and those who were blessed with wealth were to provide opportunities for the poor to work for their daily bread. Likewise, Jesus never promised wealth, but instead told us that the King of Kings had rocks for pillows and a cross to bear. He called us to follow him and seek the kingdom, and our daily needs would be provided.

Prosperity preaching holds out the American dream and says it is ours by entitlement, a godly welfare system. Health and wealth preachers promise abundance if you seed your desire by faith; give to the church and God will bless tenfold. But the accumulation of wealth fights against contentment.

Contentment is hard because all our lives we are told that new is better, more is the goal, and success is measured in material gain. The saying, *"The one who dies with the most toys wins"* will be written on many head stones, but the new saying sums up Solomon's attitude about life, *"The one who dies with the most toys-- still dies."*

Contentment is attained when we realize that everything that we have, good or bad, comes from God. When we understand that God's desire is for our best we are able to be satisfied with what He gives. We find rest in knowing that God works all things together for good to those who love Him. Therefore, whatever the circumstances God is working them for good. When we forget that God is in control we take matters into our own hands, trying to secure our future, and in doing so we either forget God or dishonor His name.

Agur's prayer raises some questions that need to be addressed. What does it mean to be satisfied with God? Does being content with God mean mediocrity and complacency? What would happen if this prayer came true in my life?

Further Reflection

1. What do you consider to the minimum size house you could live in?
2. How much do really think you could live on and be happy?
3. If you were content with less, how could you be a blessing to others?
4. How has your financial past shaped your thinking about attitude toward money?
5. What do you think would happen to the American culture if everyone were content with what they had for a year?
6. What do you need to do to adjust your attitude toward wealth and poverty to be in line with God's?

If God Is All I Need, Who is this Lord?

In order to remain faithful Agur knew his relationship with God needed to be central. Knowing God isn't easy because we don't really comprehend what it means, and before I can rest in God's provision I need to understand Him. If God is all I need, then who is this God I serve?

The Great I Am

Before the Exodus from Egypt God made Himself known to Israel by many different names. He was known as Elohim the Creator of the world, Elshadiah the almighty, and Jehovah Jira the provider. Yet, no other name drew as much awe and fear as the name YAHWEH. Yahweh, or I AM, carries the very essence of God's nature. God said to Moses,

> *"I Am who I Am. This is what you are to say to the Israelites: 'I AM has sent me to you.'... This is my name forever, the name by which I am to be remembered from generation to generation" (Exodus 3:14 and 15 NIV).*

The name conveys the idea of self-sufficiency. There was no one before Him and there will be no one after Him. Yahweh needs no one to help or comfort Him; He loves but doesn't require love outside of Himself; He is all-powerful and doesn't need a rescuer. This was important information for the former Egyptian slaves, but we need to understand it as well.

We live in a day where man believes he is at the pinnacle of evolution. Our culture wants us to accept that we need only dream and it will become reality. We have become like the architects of Babel, trying to ascend into heaven to find God, but when we get there, instead of the almighty, transcendent God of the universe, we find only ourselves. How pitiful.

A researcher witnessed an erupting volcano on the island of Sicily and stood in awe of its power and the force of nature. He said that the volcano was omnipotent and nothing could stop its dynamism. He was right, when compared to man, and for all his intellect and skill man was impotent to stop it. But compared to God the volcano was but a festering sore oozing for a while and then healed.

God stands alone in the universe, because He stands outside of His creation. As Paul said,

> *"He is before all things, and in him all things hold together" (Colossians 1:17).*

Without Him nothing that *is* would exist. That is hard for our minds to comprehend. Our pride deceives us into believing our discoveries are new. So, we contrive hypotheses, formulate theories, and establish laws in hope that they will provide answers. Yet the answers are insufficient and man is left to wonder once again, and still he will not turn to God. Even if man accepts that God exists he wants desperately to believe that God needs him.

Yet, God doesn't need anything, not even us, and as disappointing as that may seem it is also freeing. If God doesn't need me then when he chooses to do something on my behalf then it is totally free. He doesn't need me He wants me, He doesn't have to save me, he desires to rescue, and when we come to that realization the grace of God takes on new dimensions and deeper meaning.

The Chief End Of Man

Once we come to grips with the self-existence of God we are forced to reorient our lives through the grid work of His character. When this happens we begin to understand how Solomon saw the activities of the world and concluded it was meaningless, and that life without a Creator is no more than an odd assortment of circumstances strung together by fleeting moments. Our relationship with God gives meaning to our existence, and it is for that reason Solomon concluded Ecclesiastes with this note,

> *"Here is the conclusion of the matter: Fear God and keep his commandments, for this is the whole duty of man" (Eccl. 12:13 NIV).*

God is the beginning and the end. For that reason we should start every day seeking Him. Paul said,

> *"So, whether you eat or drink or whatever you do, do it all for the glory of God" (1 Corinthians 10:31 NIV).*

We need to stop asking, "*How does this or that affect my life,*" but instead ask "*How does this or that bring glory to God*?" Easier said then done, right?

In 2008, when I lost my job, I struggled with depression. I was overwhelmed with a since of loss, loss of direction, loss of purpose, loss of significance, and a loss of hope. When we believe that the chief end of man is our own pleasure the struggles of life become overwhelming. But when we see that the chief end is God's glory we can start to put our difficulties into perspective. Placed within the context of God's glory the depth of our struggle and the intensity of our pain find cause and cure. God identifies sin as its cause and salvation as its cure; while trouble is the bedfellow of sin and God's peace its remedy. Jesus said, *"In this world you will have trouble, but I have over come the world"* (John 16:33 NIV).

Trouble and pain cloud the solution to man's predicament. It isn't easy for us to let go of our natural inclination to grasp for control. It isn't easy for us to cease struggling and let God's peace replace doubt and fear. It isn't easy, but it is necessary. Realizing that God is the only being who is self-existent is the only answer to life's dilemma. This is why Agur didn't want to forget God or to dishonor His name. Agur knew that life only had meaning in the context of God glorification, and to be truly content in life we need to live and make decisions within the same context.

Nothing Greater -- A Mystery In The Making

Ok, we know that we are to do everything for the glory of God; yet, we know that just "doing" things doesn't glorify God; it is a matter of heart. Isaiah said,

"I have more than enough of burnt offerings...Stop bringing meaningless offerings" (Isaiah 1:11-13 NIV)!

These verses create tension since God is the one who commanded animal sacrifice. The problem, however, wasn't the sacrificial system; it lay in the attitude of the people. God wants our hearts, and He wants us to seek Him because we want Him, not because we fear Him. There is probably no greater expression of this than in Philippians 3:8 (NIV),

"What is more, I consider everything a loss compared to the surpassing greatness of knowing Christ Jesus my Lord, for whose sake I have lost all things."

As we seek only God, His Spirit bares witness with our spirits that we are His children. But what does it mean to really know God? Paul said it is the most important goal in a Christian's life. There is a balance between practicing spiritual disciplines in order to know God and having a checklist of activities that "make" us spiritual. We need to pray; we need to study His Word; we need to seek Him in the quiet moments of life and in the busiest. But doing these things will not insure a personal relationship with Jesus if they are not combined with a prevailing attitude of love and obedience.

Paul said it so poignantly. We are to see everything in comparison as loss, careers, family, spouses, friends, pleasures, and even our selves. They are to be considered as garbage compared to the desire to know Jesus. Paul listed his accomplishments to illustrate what this means:

1. Circumcised on the eighth day (sign of the covenant)
2. A child of Israel

3. Of the tribe of Benjamin (which means he was a relative of King David)
4. Obeyed all the laws. If there were anything required by the law he kept it to its fullest — a Pharisee.
5. Zealous -- he persecuted the church.
6. Legalistic righteousness – faultless

He realized, however, that none of this brought him into a relationship with God. It was only through the shed blood of Jesus and the filling of the Holy Spirit that he had any hope of knowing God personally. So, he gave it all up to follow Jesus. Do you understand what that means? His religious peers rejected him. He lost any opportunity to advance economically in Israel. His family and friends most likely alienated him. They would have considered him dead. He threw it all away to know Jesus.

We lose very little in claiming the name of Jesus, at least in America. In other parts of the world the cost is much greater—even to the extent of Paul's. What have I had to give up; a little discomfort among non-believing friends; an occasional ridicule for not drinking or partying; once in a while if I am being bold in sharing the gospel someone might yell at me? As a result of having it so easy we have become complacent. We take our faith for granted, and so easily forsake worship on Sunday or the fellowship of believers for our own pleasures. Isaiah speaks to this issue when he describes Israel's ability to do the right things, yet without the right attitude,

> *"These people come near to me with their mouth and honor me with their lips, but their hearts are far from me. Their worship of me is made up only of rules taught by men" (Isaiah 29:13 NIV).*

We need to examine ourselves to find if our hearts are pure, and set aside what we think is important to take hold of Jesus. It isn't something that comes all at once. It is a process and takes time. Paul said that in order to obtain Christ we have to *"forget what is behind and straining toward what is ahead, I press on toward the goal to win the prize for which God has called us heavenward in Christ Jesus"* (Philippians 3:13-14 NIV). That is--to Know Him!

What do you need to leave behind? Have others caused you pain and you have not been able to forgive them? Is there bitterness that lingers as a result of 'past hurts'? Are you antagonistic toward the opposite sex because of a marriage gone wrong? Did you grow up in a family where love was lost and the pain of abuse has not been laid at the cross? Unless we are willing to allow the past to be forgiven, if not forgotten, there will always be a barrier in our relationship with Jesus. No one says it will be easy, but it is essential.

Our culture has trained us to expect things to happen immediately, quick and instant, but nothing good comes instantly. I read a T-shirt one day that said,

> *"The will to win is useless without the will to prepare."*

I pray that the Lord gives us the will to prepare.

First, to prepare our hearts so that all we see is Jesus, having as our goal to seek His glory in all that we do. Secondly, that we will learn to practice the disciplines of the faith -- to seek Him in prayer and in His Word.

Abiding In Christ

Our relationship with Jesus is a mystery. Understanding what it means to know God can be confusing. The concept is easier to grasp by asking people to describe what knowing God would look like. There is a difference between my earthly relationships and my relationship with God. Whether it is a relationship with my wife, my children or a close friend there is a qualitative difference. For one, I can physically see my earthly relationships. I can touch them and hear them. When I ask a question there is a response that I can discern, either audibly or subtly.

At the risk of seeming unspiritual, our relationship with God seems very lopsided. I long to see the hand of God in a mighty way like the biblical saints, but the answers to my prayers seem easily explained. The odds of the same types of illness being healed, objects being found, or the directions given me, are as likely to happen in the unbeliever's life than in mine. If you are like me you have similar thoughts. But these thoughts in no way diminish in my mind the working of the Father in my life. Nor do they dismiss the wonders He displays around me every day.

When Thomas demanded to see the pierced marks on the Savior's body before believing. Jesus answered his requests, but then gave a blessing on those like us.

> *"Jesus told him, 'Because you have seen me, you have believed; blessed are those who have not seen and yet have believed" (John 20:29 NIV).*

I have been made alive because I have been quickened by faith. I continue in my faith because the Spirit bears witness with my spirit. My relationship with the Father grows because I abide in Him and His Word. Jesus said,

> *"As the Father has loved me, so have I loved you. Now remain in my love. If you obey my commands, you will remain in my love, just as I have obeyed my Father's commands and remain in his love" (John 15:9-10 NIV).*

Our relationship with God is a matter of remaining and abiding. It is resting secure in the knowledge that what God has said is true and worth putting into practice. It is an attitude of seeking God as the chief end in our lives and understanding that it is His glory that is of utmost importance. It is putting what we think is important in proper perspective to the will of God.

This is the whole point of Agur's prayer. He did not want the possessions of this world to mask his knowledge of God. He wanted an attitude and character of life that was free from falsehood and deception. He wanted to remain steadfast in the love of the Father by remaining in Him, in both the good and bad times.

> *"Let not the wise man boast of his wisdom, or the strong man boast of his strength, or the rich man boast of his riches, but let him who boasts boast about this: That he understands and knows me, that I am the Lord, who exercises kindness, justice and righteousness on earth for in these I delight, declares the Lord" (Jeremiah 9:23,24 NIV).*

Further Reflection

1. How does God's preeminence make you feel uncomfortable?
2. What priorities do you need to submit to the preeminence of God?
3. How does God's preeminence change your perspective on life, to see everything you do as means to God's glory?
4. What hinders you relationship with Christ?
5. What discipline do you need to nurture? How will you accomplish this?
6. What activity do you need to set aside in order to better abide in Christ? How difficult will that be?
7. How does your relationship with Jesus change the perspective on your sense of worth?

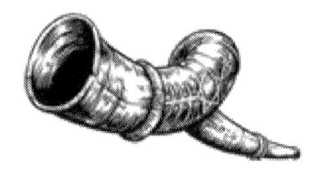

Striving For Mediocrity

Frankie Schaffer observed in his book, *Addicted to Mediocrity*, that the late 20th century culture was more interested in titillating its appetites than pursuing excellence in the arts. This satisfaction with substandard effort reflected society as a whole. The 20th century was marked by the onset of mass production, aimed at bringing to the general population, at lower costs, what only the rich had previously afforded. There was, however, a deeper motivation than just availability. The more products that could be produced at a lower cost meant more profit for the manufacturer. Quality became more of an advertising jingle than a product reality.

How many of you have bought an electronic device and had the salesman ask if you would like to buy an extended warranty? The product had built in obsolescence, and after a while it would fall apart. It's as if they are telling you,

> *"We have built a sub-standard product and if you want to pay me more money we will fix it at a later date when it falls apart."*

I call this product extortion. Hardly anyone gives a lifetime guarantee any more, but really, we are getting what we have asked for.

Apple started a revolution by providing a means to purchase electronic music over the Internet, but the sound quality diminished in order to keep the file size small enough to transfer at acceptable rates. Gone are the high fidelity sounds that echoed through quality vinyl. We want it for less, and less money means less quality — and the more we want for less the more we become addicted to mediocrity. Instamatic were substituted for single reflex cameras and Smart phones substitute the instamatic. Yet, even with the increase of mega pixels the quality of pictures have not increased, and we latch on to mediocrity because convenience, ease, and lower cost is preferred. Why is it this way, and are we, as Christians, to live differently? If we are to be content with what God gives us, does that mean we are to settle for mediocrity?

A Lazy Man

> *"If a man is lazy, the rafters sag: if his hands are idle, the house leaks"(Eccl. 10:18).*

I am not a carpenter — it's not one of my "spiritual gifts." I find that my problem is less about qualifications, and more about patiently doing quality work. Measuring, adding, cutting, fitting and sanding are not what I like to do and so I have, in many ways, become lazy. Left to me my rafters would sag.

This is not to say that I am lazy about everything,

but like everyone else we don't give 100% to everything that we do, and some things we tend to let "laziness" slip into mediocrity. What causes some people to be unconcerned with the quality of their work? Part of it comes from a culture that has taught us that instant is better and faster is more preferable. But quality doesn't come instantly or with speed. Quality comes from patient hard work.

As we become lazy our demand for quality work lessens, our appetite for more is stronger than our desire for quality. We have more T.V. shows and channels than ever before, and it is all rehash of the same stuff — and most of it is junk. Novelists pour out novels quicker than we can read them, written with the vocabulary of 7th graders so we can read them quickly and move on to the next book. The reader isn't interested in deep characters and sophisticated plots. Action, sex, and violence are preferred. As Frankie Schaffer pointed out, "we have adorned our homes with trinkets and bobbles and have called it art." We are satisfied with mediocrity because our lives are mediocre.

The Church that I pastored for 17 years struggled with the issue of mediocrity. We were often faced with doing the best we could and fitting it into our schedules. We wanted to have quality, but our efforts were less than necessary. We had a penchant for giving groups names and the group that led music for our children's program mid-week had nicknamed themselves "Close Enough." It was really a joke, because they worked hard to provide good music for the children. It began, as they were fine tuning one of the songs for the evening. The banjo player felt that they were missing a chord. They were trying to figure it out when they were told they needed to go out on stage. The leader of the group said, "That's close enough." The name stuck, and if the truth were told it would stick to most of us.

Military retirees often use the phrase, *"Good enough for government work."* These phrases are a reflection of how we often view life — 'Close Enough.' In other words God knows our failings and He is forgiving. Close enough is good enough because we usually aren't willing to give enough.

To The Glory Of God

> *"Whatever your hand finds to do, do it with all your might, for in the grave, where you are going, there is neither working nor planning nor knowledge nor wisdom" (Eccl. 9:10 NIV).*

Laziness is not an option for Christians. It goes against everything that God has recreated us for. The writer of Ecclesiastes said that whatever we find for our hands to do we are to do it with all our might. Our culture and our desires don't set the standard; God's glory sets the standard.

> *"So whether you eat or drink or whatever you do, do it all for the glory of God" (1 Corinthians 10:31 NIV).*

Our work is a reflection of God's glory, because we are a

reflection of God' work. When we do a job, a project, or anything else with less effort than we are capable then we have not done it to the glory of God. Paul explained it this way,

> *"Whatever you do, work at it with all your heart, as working for the Lord, not for men, since you know that you will receive an inheritance from the Lord as a reward. It is the Lord Christ you are serving" (Colossians 3:23, 24 NIV).*

First, we must understand what is our motivation for work. Jesus said that He is always with us, and He sent the Holy Spirit to live within us. So, no matter what we are doing He is watching and working. This is one of the most important lessons we need to learn as believers, and yet, one of the hardest.

In college I was employed at a merchandizing warehouse for an amusement park. I worked with two other young men, and our job was to place stuffed animals into plastic bags. We did this for eight to ten hours a day. The men I worked with took quite a few unscheduled breaks. The work area was in a corner of the building and out of the sight of our supervisor, and, you know, it didn't matter. Not really, in the long run. Who cared if we bagged a thousand in a day or fifteen hundred? Would it affect their profits? No, but that wasn't the point. So, as I continued working they came to despise me. They would say, "Slow down, you're making us look bad." I wanted to respond; "No, you're doing that on your own." Instead I merely said that I was doing what I was paid to do. My Christian values wouldn't allow me to take advantage of my employer because at the heart of every job I am really working for my master—Jesus.

Ted Engstrum in his book, *Pursing Excellence*, described the pursuit of God's glory not as a comparison with others but a comparison with ourselves. He said that the pursuit of excellence is doing a job a little better than we did the time before. The pursuit of excellence implies a standard by which I can measure my progress. So, if I am working in carpentry I need to know what the standards are so I can pursue excellence. The same is true in our spiritual lives. If we are to pursue a life that is excellent and glorifying to God we need to know what our standard is, and the Scriptures make it clear.

> *"Your attitude should be the same as that of Christ Jesus..." (Philippians 2:5 NIV).*

> *"Husbands love your wives, just as Christ loved the church, and gave Himself up for her" (Ephesians 5:25 NIV).*

> *"Be perfect, therefore, as your heavenly Father is perfect" (Matthew 5:48).*

God is our standard; therefore we measure ourselves, not by the standards of the world, but by the character of God. This, however, raises a troubling question: Are we to be perfect?

Jesus' admonition toward perfection wasn't what we think. Jesus was talking in the context of our love for others, those we know and those who are our enemies. He tells us that our love for others is to be complete and full. Our love is to include all people, as did God's love through Jesus. Our love is to be all encompassing. That is impossible if not for the Spirit of God in our lives

The Scripture never teaches that we are to reach perfection, though we are to strive for it.

"Not that I have already obtained all this, or have already been made perfect, but I press on to take hold of that for which Christ Jesus took hold of me" (Philippians 3:12 NIV).

Paul wouldn't have considered himself perfect, but he knew that God had called him to be something more than what he was. His pursuit to be like Jesus was life long, and he measured his behavior according the standard of Jesus' character. As we pursue excellence and put away laziness we take the life of Christ as our guide. The Word of God, both written and living, is to be the measure by which we conduct our lives.

To Live Lives Of Contentment

What does any of this have to do with living lives of contentment? As I read and studied Agur's prayer this question came to my mind:

> *"Does contentment breed laziness, and does it exclude pursuing excellence?"*

We are called to be content with what we have, and we are called to rest in the Lord and satisfied with what He gives. If this is true do I need to pursue excellence in my job? Can I do so-so work and be content with whatever I accomplish? Isn't being a Christian more than just being polished and perfect? The answer to these questions is both yes and no.

YES — It is interesting that in every text I could find where God talks about being content the context is money. As Paul says, *"The love of money is the root of all kinds of evil."* Therefore we are to be content with what God gives us. We are to be satisfied if we are in want or if we want for nothing. God is the source of good and evil and we are to find our rest in Him.

NO — But that doesn't mean that we should sit back and do nothing. God has given us gifts, and Paul says that we are to pursue our goal. Solomon says to do everything with all our might. These are words of action not passivity. Doing all for the glory of God is to go the extra mile. The question of perfection isn't in the picture. The bottom line is this — We are to pursue God's glory in everything that we do and be content with what He gives us.

Every Sunday I struggled with the number of people who were in attendance. I could have taken the view that whatever God gave would be enough for me, and then do nothing to improve the way I preached, or make sure that the words were correct on the screen, or the praise team was on tune and the drama people were good. We could be 'content' with who comes in the doors and not be friendly or caring or loving. That is absurd; no one would condone that attitude.

Instead I needed to improve the delivery of my

messages and show its relevance to the culture. Our praise team needed to pursue excellence (within the talent that God had given), our drama team needed to look as if they had practiced, and so on. Then, as I look at the numbers I could be content with who God brought. I needed to work as if it all depended on me knowing that nothing I did made a difference without the working of the Holy Spirit.

If I believed that it all depended on my abilities I could never be content, because I am not perfect. I would always be striving and worrying, wondering if I would ever be successful. Knowing that I am not perfect, as I do my best and try to improve, I can be content with the knowledge that God is in control, and He will accomplish His work in His time. Isn't that what contentment is, resting in the providence of God and being thankful for what He has given me? So, work hard, pursue excellence and be content in what God gives.

> *"So neither he who plants nor he who waters is anything, but only*

God, who makes things grow... If any man builds on this (Jesus) foundation using gold, silver, costly stones, wood, hay, or straw, his work will be shown for what it is, because the DAY will bring it light. It will be revealed with fire, and the fire will test the quality of each man's work" (1 Corinthians 3:7,12,13 NIV).

Further Reflection

1. What areas of your life do you tend to relax your standards?
2. How have you experienced other people who have slipped into mediocrity?
3. How has your spiritual life been less then robust?
4. What do you need to work on so that you can be a person who pursues excellence?
5. Why is contentment difficult?
6. What do you need to do to rest in God's provision and be content in Him?

Running With The Big Dogs

What boy hasn't dreamed of going to the stars? The allure of space travel and exploring the galaxy captures the imagination. My dream of being an astronaut, however, would only be lived vicariously through the efforts of the Apollo Space missions and my favorite T.V. shows. I would watch them over and over again pretending to be one of the crew. Maybe that's why my dream changed from actually wanting to be an astronaut to being an actor. If I couldn't go to space I would live it out on the stage.

My first theatre class started with the immortal saying, "The world is a stage." The bright lights, the roar of the crowd, and the adulation of the audience thrust this young thespian to seek center stage, but it never happened. Like my dream of space travel changed with time, my acting career was side lined by the grace of God. Swept up by His mercy and love I exchanged dazzling oratory for the simple message of the gospel. There is little fame in the trenches of ministry, and few ever make it into the limelight.

Yet, God does raise up a few to lead the charge in the battle for the Kingdom. They were men who never saw themselves as great, but greatness was thrust on them because they were uncompromising in their stand for God. They would not deviate from the message of Christ. Peter said to Jesus,

> *"Lord, to whom shall we go? You have the words of eternal life. We believe and know that you are the Holy One of God" (John 6:67-69 NIV).*

Fame can be a devastating bedfellow. Many people caught in the light of its glory are blinded to the light of God's glory. We see the wreckage throughout the Christian music industry. Men and women parade themselves in front of the world singing and dancing to the glory of God while their private lives are falling apart. Athletes' instant stardom and weak faith create poor role models for young Christians seeking to follow Jesus.

Yet, I know that pedestals are not just for those in the spotlight of national acclaim. Every Sunday, around the world, men stand before congregations eagerly seeking a word from the Lord. Their rapt attention to the words of the preacher can create a false sense of importance. It amazes me each time I say something from the pulpit or in a classroom and someone takes notes. Who am I that anyone would listen to me? I must be someone; they are taking notes! Pride begins to rear it ugly head.

Making a difference runs deep in those who preach and teach the gospel. There are times I want to be like Billy Graham—impacting the world! Yet, I realize my world may consist of only 35,000 people or 3,200, of which I will only connect with a few. I have often prayed, "God allow me to impact one life that will impact a thousand." Alas, even in that prayer I can hear the faint call of fame.

This brings us back to Agur's prayer. Who was Agur? We really don't know. He may have been well known in his time, but in ours he is lost between the great proverbs of the Bible. Yet, he brings to us two simple requests that are the most important appeals we could ever bring before the Lord: a godly character and a life of contentment. Through the simple preaching of faithful men God builds His Kingdom. Yes, God uses the giants of the faith, but He also uses the foot soldiers to carry on the fight. God loves to use the simple things to confuse the wise.

> *"I will destroy the wisdom of the wise; the intelligence of the intelligent I will frustrate" (1 Corinthians 1:19).*

Intelligence and wisdom are important, but if they lead us away from God they are as dung. This gives me hope that God will use someone like me as I seek Him in honest humility. Each morning is an opportunity to touch someone's life for the gospel. Each day is a new morning of God's mercy and grace. Each evening is a time of rest in God's strength and assurance. All this is mine whether anyone notices me or not.

Sometimes I wonder if people like Agur, Jabez, and Onesiphorus ever thought they would impact the world as they have? It is the simple things that we do for Jesus that have the greatest impact for eternity. Jesus doesn't expect us to be a Paul or a Peter; rather He wants us to see every moment as an opportunity to serve Him.

> *"The King will reply, 'I tell you the truth, whatever you did for one of the least of these brothers of mine, you did for me'" (Matthew 25:40).*

Did Agur seek fame and fortune? Did Jabez expect to sell the latest books on his prayer? Did any of these men realize that they would be famous? You know, I don't think they cared. All these men wanted to do was serve their Lord. I don't want to make them out to be more than just men, but I do believe that their desire was for God to work His will in their lives.

It is a lesson our celebrity driven culture needs to learn. As believers we need to go back to the roots of our faith and honor the servant above others—the least shall be called great. This malady isn't unique to our society. The disciples argued over who would be the greatest in the kingdom; they wanted the seat of honor; they wanted to be in charge; and what does Jesus tell them?

> *"If anyone wants to be first, he must be the very last, and the servant of all" (Mark 9:35).*

In 2014 the Pope astounded the world. Instead of hiding himself apart from the people he took to the streets to serve. The contrast of power and majesty bowing before the needy and calling the saints to humility is so contrary to the world that the world couldn't stop talking about it.

To put on the mind of Jesus is to put on an apron and serve others. This isn't an issue of talent, gifting, or abilities; it is a matter of obedience and life style. We are to put others before ourselves and think of their needs before our own. Easy? Not on your life! Is it contrary to our culture? Definitely! Is it powerful and life changing? Absolutely!

When we put on godly character and learn the secret to contentment we will seek glory and honor only for our Lord and Savior. We will not seek ourselves first, but put others first. We will not long for the applause and adulation of the crowd, but simply long for the words of our Lord:

> *"Well done, good and faithful servant! You have been faithful with few things; I will put you in charge of many things. Come and share your master's happiness" (Matthew 25:23).*

Further Reflection

1. Have you ever thought, "No one appreciates what I do at church."

2. How has service become drudgery?

3. If you are a behind the scenes person have you ever felt used?

4. What do you need to do for the least of these our brothers?
5. If no one ever noticed your work for the Lord how would that make you feel?

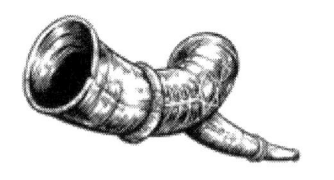

If All I Had Were God

The snow was falling; the flakes grew larger as they reached the ground, and they fell in stark contrast to the billowing smoke coming from the house. I stood with the owners as they watched their home go up in flames. Fortunately they had insurance, but it would never replace the memories or their dog.

For many people this would have been an overwhelming and devastating event. Yet, this couple had a strong faith, and a clear understanding between the temporal and eternal. Standing in front of the house, the heat reminded me of Peter's description of the last days:

"But the day of the

Lord will come like a thief. The heavens will disappear with a roar; the elements will be destroyed by fire, and the earth and everything in it will be laid bare" (1 Peter 3:9).

The Scriptures talk a lot about obedience, judgment, loss, and reward. In America we speak about God's reward for those who believe, but we don't like to talk about bad and sad things. We have Christianized Nietzsche (the philosopher who coined the phrase 'God is dead'). Nietzsche said that pain is a natural part of life, but that it hasn't a place in meaningful existence. Therefore, pain should be avoided for the greater aim of enjoying life (Beyond Good and Evil). American Christians reword it this way,

"There is no greater aim for man than to be blessed by God with long life, total happiness, and free from pain."

We want to believe that as a result of our faith in Christ that judgment, punishment, and consequences have all been eradicated. Of course, that's not what the

Bible says. Jesus said that there would be trouble. Peter said that we are to endure suffering. James said suffering produces character. We don't talk about suffering much because if we did, who would want to become a believer? So we package it in our 21st century, Madison Avenue, made for T.V. way and hope that people will buy our brand of religion over someone else's.

Affluence and freedom from pain should never be our goal. We follow Jesus because there is no other way that leads to the Father. The road is narrow and few will find it. We need to preach that without God in Christ there is nothing else. It is Christ who holds everything together and without Him nothing exists (Colossians 1:17).

If everything is going to burn as Peter said, then it is important to know what is temporal and what is eternal. When we talked about excellence we emphasized the need to build on solid foundations. I think it would be good to reemphasize what Paul said,

"If any man builds on this foundation using gold, silver, costly stones, wood, hay or straw, his work will be shown for what it is, because the Day will bring it to light it will be revealed with fire, and the fire will test the quality of each man's work. If what he has built survives, he will receive his reward. If it is burned up, he will suffer loss; he himself will be saved, but only as one escaping through the flames" (1 Corinthians 3:7-13).

I don't want to enter heaven with only scorched pants! I want to find out what will last forever. Understanding what lasts forever will guide me in how to spend my time, what is worth my effort, and what will be pleasing to God.

I love the passages in Scripture that talk of Jesus' transfiguration, the day he allowed Peter, James and John a glimpse of His glory. Jesus asked Peter, James and John to wait and pray as He went a little further along the path. As Jesus prayed His appearance changed. He shone like white light and with Him stood two men, Moses and Elijah. These men represented the law and the prophets, and they stood with Jesus discussing with him His impending death.

When Peter and his friends woke they became excited, and as usual tried to figure out what they should do. Peter thought they could make something, booths, for these important men. He was totally distracted from what was important, and franticly tried to keep busy, and characteristically he chose the wrong course of action.

The Father's voice broke through the confusion and refocused the disciples. *"This is my Son, whom I love; with Him I am well pleased. Listen to Him" (Luke 9:35)!* Don't run around, don't build, don't talk—listen! Not to Moses, not to Elijah, only to Jesus. Why? Because He is my son!

What was their response? They fell to the ground in fear. They were terrified and they took a position of submission. They thought their lives were over, because they had heard the voice of God. God's voice thundered as of old, the voice of glory, justice and law. But it was Jesus who touched these panic stricken men. He didn't chastise them. He didn't condemn them, but in grace and mercy he touched them and told them not to be afraid.

That's what I want! There is plenty of condemnation and judgment. What I desperately need is God's grace. I need to have the touch of Jesus in my life. I need to know that I am loved beyond the measure of what I deserve. I want to know that when everything is burned up I will not be lost to the flames of eternal judgment. I need to know Jesus.

Matthew paints a wonderful picture as he relates this marvelous story. He ends with what we all need:

> *"When they looked up, they saw no one except Jesus" (Matt 17:8).*

That is the reality of life. When we finally look

up all we will see is Jesus. The question is will we come to this conclusion now or later, in the days of decision or the days of judgment? If we choose now to follow Jesus, to see nothing but Him, then we will put our lives in order and build with gold and silver. If we wait, then we will build with nothing but straw and hay and we will feel loss. I love this verse from an old hymn,

> *"Turn your eyes upon Jesus Look full in His wonderful face and the things of earth will grow strangely dim in the light of His glory and grace" (Helen H. Lemmel, 1922)*

It's All About Jesus

It's all about God. I truly believe this. At times it is difficult to live it practically because every day business gets in the way--good things, helpful things, but often times not the most important things. I am often frustrated as I struggle to maintain a life that is filled with the glory of God. Yet, one thing is for sure, I know it is all about God.

With this

perspective I can live a life that is pleasing to Him, and so can you. When you come to realize that it is all about God everything else is put into its proper perspective. When Agur asked God for godly character and contentment, he was acknowledging that it is all about God. If he did not believe that, then why would he care about being kept from lies and deceit? If it weren't about God then we would seek the pleasures of this life to make us happy. If lies and deceit can achieve physical pleasure, personal gain, and power then we should lie even more.

But if it is all about God, then we view our relationships differently, our possessions differently, and our time differently. If it is all about God then my frustration with my wife is put into perspective, my children's moodiness isn't the end of the world, and the authorities over me are due my respect. When I lose focus on whom it is all about I allow my selfish ambition to run amuck, I turn to the wrong places for answers when pressure bears down on me, and I chose to spend time in personal pursuits and not in the pursuit of Him who gives me true rest, peace, and joy.

I don't know what tomorrow will bring. Will my house burn down? Will my wife leave me? Will one of my children die? Will everything be taken away? Job faced these very things and struggled with God and how to respond. In the end God spoke to him and refocused his perspective. As a result this is what Job said,

> *"My ears had heard of you but now my eyes have seen you. Therefore I despise myself and repent in dust and ashes" (Job 42:5,6).*

He finally understood that it's all about God.

Further Reflection

1. How has the church made it about something else other than God?

2. How has the pursuit of the American dream kept you from focusing on God?

3. What have you allowed to set itself up as a barrier between you and Jesus?

4. If you could give up one thing in order to free up time for God's service, what would it be?

5. What does God have to do to get your attention so that all you will see is Jesus?

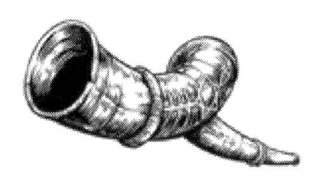

A Final Word

The road to the heavenly city is filled with joys and difficulties. The way is marked with temptations and victories. Coming to grips with what is important in life is the key to perseverance. There are no formulas, there are no quick fixes or gimmicks, but what we have is a guide in both the written Word and the living Word of God. It's a matter of trusting the author of life, that He knows what is best, good, and perfect. We need to seek Him in prayer and the study of His Word. It is this task of persevering to the end, of hearing the welcoming words of our Savior, and to living in the blessed hope that I pray along with Agur,

TWO THINGS I ASK OF YOU
DENY THEM NOT TO ME BEFORE I DIE
REMOVE FAR FROM ME FALSEHOOD AND LYING
GIVE ME NEITHER POVERTY NOR RICHES
FEED ME WITH THE FOOD THAT IS NEEDFUL FOR ME
LEST I BE FULL AND DENY YOU
AND SAY, "WHO IS THE LORD?"
OR LEST IS BE POOR AND STEAL
AND PROFANE THE NAME OF MY GOD

PROVERBES 30:7-9

Made in the USA
Columbia, SC
06 March 2018